Text © 2009 Prism Publications, Inc.

Written by the editors of *Traverse, Northern Michigan's Magazine:*
Elizabeth Edwards, Jeff Smith, Lynda Twardowski and Emily Betz Tyra
Designed by Kelly Nogoski

Prism Publications, Inc.
148 E. Front St.
Traverse City, MI 49684
231-941-8174
MyNorth.com

ISBN: 0-918293-08-1

Published by Prism Publications, Inc., which also publishes the periodicals:
*Traverse, Northern Michigan's Magazine; Northern Home & Cottage; MyNorth
Vacation Guide; MyNorth Wedding.* Other books published by Prism Publications
include *Reflections of a Life Up North,* by Deborah Wyatt Fellows and *The Cottage
Cookbook.*

This book is available at MyNorth.com or by calling 231-941-8174.

Booksellers wishing to order wholesale quantities of this book may email inquiries to
books@traversemagazine.com.

101

ways

to 💗

TRAVERSE CITY

Sail
the freshwater sea

1

Unleash some sea shanties aboard Grand Traverse Bay's majestic schooner, *Manitou,* which offers freshwater sailing **adventures** ranging from two hours to four days. 231-941-2000, TALLSHIPSAILING.COM.

tc
baseball

Secure a seat in the sun (first base side) for a good old-fashioned **home game** of the Traverse City **Beach Bums.** Fireworks at many of the Friday games. 333 STADIUM DRIVE, 231-943-0100, TRAVERSECITYBEACHBUMS.COM.

2

3 brew
TOUR

Take a T.C. microbrew tour! Self-guided stops at **Mackinaw Brewing Co.** (161 E. FRONT ST.), **Right Brain Brewery** (221 GARLAND ST.), **North Peak Brewing Co.** (400 W. FRONT ST.) and **Jolly Pumpkin Old Mission** (13512 PENINSULA DR.) with plenty of snacks—and naps—along the way. FOR TIPS VISIT MYNORTH.COM/LINKS.

Regatta
WATCH-SPOT

Snack on smoked whitefish pâté and **sip** Bahama mamas around the tiki bar at **Scott's Harbor Grill,** the best seat in town for watching spinnakers fly during Grand Traverse Yacht Club's Wednesday evening races.

12719 BAY SHORE DR., 231-922-2114, SCOTTSHARBORGRILL.COM.

5 *dune* CLIMB

Many attempt the Dune Climb at the **Sleeping Bear Dunes.** But only the bravest complete the entire thigh-burning rite of passage: climb and descend a series of steep sand mountains until, at last, you hit the reviving **blue oasis** of Lake Michigan. Round trip is about 3.5 miles and may take 3 hours, but you can eat two waffle cones at **The Cherry Republic** in Glen Arbor afterward, no regrets.

NPS.GOV/SLBE/.

Blueberry pick at Buchan's Blueberry Hill, **Old Mission Peninsula.** Make it even more of a thrill and approach the farm from the east, via Nelson Road, a rambling **sun-speckled** dirt two-track off M-37. Once home, put your plunder into blueberry purses, recipe on MyNorth.com (CLICK FOOD & WINE, CHOOSE RECIPES). Monday–Saturday. 1472 NELSON RD., 231-223-4846.

berry
picking
6

Take home the very **best bottle** from each of the seven wineries on **Old Mission Peninsula.** Plot a seven-course wine dinner to serve your very best friends. WINERIESOFOLDMISSION.COM.

WAREHOUSE DISTRICT

True, there are only a handful of warehouses in the TC Warehouse District. But, Garland Street is about quality-footage not square-footage. **Right Brain Brewery**—flavors strong, clean, inventive. **Cuppa Joe**—comfortably enchanting café-chat ambiance. **Inside Out Gallery**—performances on stage, art on walls. **West Bay Antiques**—lots (and lots) o' stuff. **Boardman Paddle & Pedal**—rent fun now.

INTERLOCHEN
Arts Academy

Take in a national musical act, or be moved by the young and **extraordinary talent** of the prodigies of Interlochen Summer Arts Camp at the sell-out Collage event, all in the **open-air** Kresge Auditorium. 4000 HWY M-137 SOUTH, INTERLOCHEN, 231-276-7200, INTERLOCHEN.ORG.

Cheesecake **and a walk**

Stroll the **lawns** of the Grand Traverse Commons (formerly Traverse City State Hospital) with a frozen cheesecake-on-a-stick you snag at **Underground Cheesecake Company.** Look for the little lemony-colored brick building on Yellow Dr. 231-929-4418, UNDERGROUNDCHEESECAKE.COM.

10

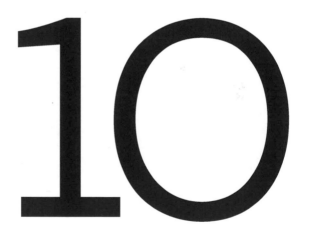

11

b●wl

A dark cloud over Traverse City? Bring on the bowling at **Wilderness Crossing.**

1355 SILVER LAKE CROSSINGS BLVD., 231-943-0893,

WILDERNESSCROSSING.COM.

CRYSTAL
mountain

Slip into your own luge-style **sled** and maneuver Crystal Mountain Coaster's tracks as they **curve and dip** 1,600 feet down the ski hill. Control your own speed—it's no kiddy ride if you go full tilt. The lift ride to the mountaintop is a blast, too. CRYSTALMOUNTAIN.COM

12

Roadside
fruit markets

Cruise up **Fruit Stand Alley**—Take U.S. 31 north out of TC along the Lake Michigan coast, and find a **gold mine** of roadside fruit markets. Find out what's **cream of the crop** at each. (Folks are such fans of the piecrust at Royal Farms, the baker rolls out extra to shape into snail cookies with cinnamon and sugar). ROYALFARMSINC.COM.

13

14

petting zoo

The petting zoo at **Black Star Farms** in Suttons Bay is abuzz with lambs, llamas, pot-bellied pigs, baby bunnies. Have you ever seen **a baby mini horse?** 10844 E. REVOLD RD., SUTTONS BAY, BLACKSTARFARMS.COM.

15

leelanau WINE TASTING

Wine taste through Leelanau County, where 21 **wineries** pepper the **rolling landscape.** Pick a theme like Rieslings, fruit wines, bubblies or reds. LPWINES.COM.

dog
jump contest

Watch pooch athletes perform incredible dock **jumps** at the National Cherry Festival's **Ultimate Air Dog Competition.** Fest begins first Saturday of July.

800-968-3380, CHERRYFESTIVAL.ORG.

16

17

Peshawbestown
POW WOW

Be a part of one of the longest running **festivals** in the North at The Grand Traverse Band of **Ottawa and Chippewa Indians'** Peshawbestown Pow Wow, every August. 866-534-7750, GTBINDIANS.ORG.

18

schooner festival

Grand Traverse Bay is a **back-in-time** vision as more than a dozen schooners and sloops **set sail** at summer's end for Traverse City's Schooner Festival. At Open Space park and Clinch Marina. 231-946-2647, MICHIGANSCHOONERFESTIVAL.ORG.

State Theatre

Come nightfall, shoot for the **stars:** a twinkling ceiling—plus ushers in spiffy uniforms, free **popcorn** Tuesdays, super-cush seating, classic red-curtain raising and the sweetest sound system around—awaits at the **historic** State Theatre. 233 E. FRONT ST., 231-947-4800, STATETHEATRETC.ORG.

20

mini golf

Putt your way through caves, around moats, over bridges and **past pirate ships** at Pirates Cove mini golf. 1710 U.S. 31 N., 231-938-9599, PIRATESCOVE.NET.

orchard blossom viewing

Drive up **Old Mission Peninsula** during **cherry** blossom season. Mid-May, the hills of this orchard-covered peninsula are awash in **pink and white** blossoms.

21

22

Pulled Pork Sandwich. THE COOKS' HOUSE, 439 E. FRONT ST., 231-946-8700. J&S Hamburg. 302 W. FRONT ST., 231-947-5500. Cherries Moobilee Ice Cream. MOOMERS, 7263 N. LONG LAKE RD. 231-941-4122. Leelanau Cheese Co. Raclette. BLACK STAR FARMS, 10844 E. REVOLD RD., (SUTTONS BAY), 231-271-2600. Crumb Topped Cherry Pie. GRAND TRAVERSE PIE COMPANY, 525 W. FRONT ST., 231-922-7437. Early Glow Strawberry Preserves. AMERICAN SPOON FOODS, 230 E. FRONT ST., 231-935-4480. Whitefish pâté. BURRITT'S MARKET. 509 W. FRONT ST., 231-946-3300. Parmesan Olive Herb Bread. PLEASANTON BRICK OVEN BAKERY, 812 COTTAGE VIEW DR., THE VILLAGE AT GRAND TRAVERSE COMMONS, 231-941-1964. The Fungus Amongus sandwich. FOLGARELLI'S ITALIAN IMPORT MARKET, 424 W. FRONT ST., 231-941-7651. Prime Rib. BOONE'S LONG LAKE INN. 7208 SECOR RD., 231-946-3991.

MUST EATS

Discover
a new beach

The Traverse City area abounds with beaches from secluded niches to Malibu-style sands bustling with bronze bods. Choose where to **spend your day in the sun** at MyNorth.com. GO TO OUTDOORS, BEACHES.

23

24

HOMETOWN
ice cream

Long Lake's **long-loved dairy farm** and ice cream oasis, Moomers, was voted **best in the country** in *Good Morning America's* Best Scoops Contest. See why with a scoop of one of their 101 homemade creamery concoctions—black walnut, apple crisp, fresh apricot, or **cherries moobilee.** Say hi to Bessie out back. 7263 N. LONG LAKE RD., 231-941-4122.

DRIVE-IN *diner*

The lights of **Don's Drive-In** lure people cruising along East Grand Traverse Bay and campers from the nearby 342-site Traverse City State Park. Snag a parking spot at a 2-way speaker. It's a good day when a Don's **real-fruit malt** is on your horizon, whirred with raspberries, strawberries, or—when in Rome—juicy cherries. 2030 U.S. 31 N., 231-938-1860.

25

26

Canoeing AND horseback riding

Explore the Northwoods by **saddle or paddle** at Ranch Rudolf, a sprawling Western-style ranch that offers guided horseback trail rides and canoe trips down the **beautifully wild** Boardman River. 6841 BROWN BRIDGE RD., 231-947-9529, RANCHRUDOLF.COM.

27

CLINCH PARK

Check out the boats in the marina, spread your feast on a picnic table or stretch out on **1,500 feet of sand.** You'll find lifeguards on duty and public restrooms from mid-June through August at this **watery Nirvana.** GRANDVIEW PARKWAY AT THE FOOT OF UNION ST.

An ideal family beach
tucked away off M-37 at the
base of Old Mission Peninsula
where Garfield and Grandview
Parkway intersect, Bryant Park
is outfitted with a playground,
restrooms, grills, and lifeguards
from mid-June through August.

bryant park

28

29

BEACH VOLLEYBALL

Wear nothing but a bathing suit, but don't forget your attack spike when you head to the volleyball **sand courts** at West End Beach, equipped with six nets, well maintained courts, and big blue **West Grand Traverse Bay** to cool off in. Pick-up games nightly.

GRANDVIEW PARKWAY JUST WEST OF UNION STREET.

Hop on your bike for an easy spin on this paved 8.5-mile **biking, walking and inline skating** path that gets you close enough to West and East Grand Traverse Bay to **stop for dips** along the way.

231-941-4300, TRAVERSETRAILS.ORG.

TART trail

30

Pick your own cherries at **Edmondson Orchard and the Cherry Connection** on Old Mission Peninsula. Take Center Road (M-37) 8.5 miles north of Traverse City until you see the yellow gazebo and fruit stand on the east (right) side of the road. Cherry season is July and into August. 231-223-7130.

U-PICK *cherries*

31¢

32

national *cherry*
festival

Air shows, carnival rides, cherry pie eating con-
tests, parades, fireworks and way more—the
eight-day National Cherry Festival is
**Traverse City's toast to its title
as the cherry capital of the
world.** Beginning every summer on the first
Saturday of July. 800-968-3380, CHERRYFESTIVAL.ORG.

33

Fresh asparagus

Late May through mid-June, brake for asparagus at Norconk's self-serve asparagus stand on the south side of M-72 about 7 miles west of Traverse City. The **tender green stalks** are fresh in from the nearby **Norconk farm.**

Friday Night
LIVE

Traverse City's downtown vibe ramps up to a carnival atmosphere for Friday Night Live, a block party that fills the 100 and 200 blocks of E. Front Street (closed to traffic for the event) with musicians, magicians, food vendors and other family fun. FRIDAYS, 5:30 P.M. TO 9 P.M., LATE JULY THROUGH AUGUST. 231-922-2050, DOWNTOWNTC.COM.

34

OLD MISSION
bike tour

This **classic ride** to the tip of Old Mission is a must do for two-wheel devotees. Start at the base of Old Mission Peninsula, **follow the east shore** northward (Get a map and stay off Center Road as long as possible). When you reach the **lighthouse** at the tip, follow Peninsula Drive back down the peninsula's west side. Orchards. Hills. Water. Right on.

36
Little Italy, TC

Boutiques, coffee shops and eateries that make you feel like you're in an Italian piazza. It's all in **the Mercato, at Building 50,** the Victorian Italianate main building at the **historic** Village at Grand Traverse Commons. 231-941-1900, THEVILLAGETC.COM.

37
TC LIBRARY

You can borrow **books, DVD's and CD's galore** at the Traverse Area District Library, but you can also watch Cinema Curiosa's avant-garde **films,** hear **live music** or face off on a **video-game big screen.** Got tots? Bring 'em to Wiggler's **story hour** or explore the **children's gardens** out back. 231-932-8500, TADL.ORG.

FARMERS MARKET

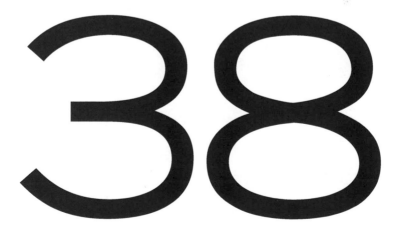

Wednesdays and Saturdays early summer to late fall, farmers back up their trucks to the blue awnings beside the Boardman River for the Traverse City Farmers Market. Their goods, including **produce, honey, flowers, baked goods and more,** are all fresh from the region's verdant hills. 8 A.M. TO 2 P.M., SATURDAYS, EARLY APRIL TO EARLY DECEMBER; AND 8 A.M. TO 1 P.M., WEDNESDAYS, MAY THROUGH OCTOBER.

38

Drive 17 breathtaking miles up **Old Mission Peninsula** to its tip, where you'll find Lighthouse Park, a dreamy castaway beach backed by a forest full of hiking trails. Don't miss the **historic** log cabin and the 1870-built Old Mission Point Lighthouse, a prim white **beacon of Great Lakes history** that's open daily for self-guided tours. OLDMISSION.COM.

39

LIGHTHOUSE
charm

40

Old-fashioned TREATS

Step through the creaky screen door at the **Old Mission General Store,** buy candy for a penny, sip a cup of nickel coffee and poke around for **old-fashioned essentials** like red woolen long underwear and Beemans gum. Find it on Mission Road near the peninsula's end. 231-223-4310.

41

DENNOS
MUSEUM

Eclectic and sophisticated, the Dennos Museum Center features interesting **exhibits,** fine permanent collections (including an array of Inuit art) and **entertainment** in Milliken Auditorium. Families shouldn't miss the **Discovery Gallery,** with its hands-on art and science stuff. 1701 E. FRONT ST., 231-995-1055, DENNOSMUSEUM.ORG.

fishtown

The **weathered fishing shanties** of Leland's Fishtown honor this watery region's fishing heritage; the funky boutiques that fill them are as hip as the season. **Watch boats** chug in and out of the harbor. Buy **whitefish** smoked right there. In Leland, 27 miles northwest of Traverse City. PRESERVINGFISHTOWN.ORG.

42

dune drive

The 7.5-mile **Pierce Stocking Scenic Drive** winds atop the Sleeping Bear Dunes, 450 feet above Lake Michigan. Expect **see-forever lookouts** and intimate landscape. Sleeping Bear Dunes National Lakeshore, M-109 between Glen Arbor and Empire, about 25 miles west of Traverse City. 231-326-5134, NPS.GOV/SLBE.

43

44

HORSE SHOWS by the Bay

The nation's **premier equestrians** and their gorgeous mounts compete in dressage, hunter and jumpers events at the Horse Shows by the Bay Equestrian Festival. **The multi-week summer event** is held at Flintfields Horse Park, 80-acres outfitted with 1,000 stalls, five show rings, a spectator pavilion and a boutique campground. 231-267-3700, HORSESHOWSBYTHEBAY.COM.

JACOB'S
corn maze

Wander a **labyrinth of towering corn** stalks at Jacob's Corn Maze. Also a half-acre "Super Freak" **pumpkin patch.** Weekends from August 23 to November 1. (Fright Nights around Halloween.) M-72, 3.5 MILES WEST OF TC, 231-632-6293, JACOBS-CORN-MAZE.COM.

45

46

Escape
to an old-timey cottage

Turn back the clock to an **unplugged vacation** where wi-fi and cable don't necessarily come with, but amenities do include bonfire pits and a line to dry swimsuits and towels. RENT AN UP NORTH COTTAGE AT MYNORTH.COM. GO TO VACATION, RENT A COTTAGE.

47

NMC **BBQ**

Born in 1956, the Northwestern Michigan College Barbecue long ago became Traverse City's big, **family springtime cookout.** Tasty **buffalo burgers;** proceeds benefit the college.

MAIN CAMPUS, MID-MAY, NMC.EDU/BBQ/.

Opera House

Thirty years of work and $8.5 million have uplifted the spirit and restored the beauty of the 1892 City Opera House, the oldest Victorian opera house in Michigan. Check the show line-up. 106 E. FRONT ST., 231-941-8082, CITYOPERAHOUSE.ORG.

Catch trout in the Boardman River

H_2O that's clean, cool and swift has earned the Boardman River a **Blue Ribbon Trout Stream** label. **Wade or float** for the wily browns and brookies yourself. Honor some flyfishing history by casting at Mayfield Pond, where Len Halladay invented the world-renowned Adams fly.

49

50

EXPLORE THE *Northwoods*

Lace up your walking shoes and lose yourself in the Northwoods. To make sure you get back home in time for dinner, find your trail at MyNorth.com. GO TO OUTDOORS, HIKE.

51

Cherry Bowl
DRIVE-IN

Settle in with your family or your honey for a **summer night** at a drive-in movie theater. The Cherry Bowl ramps up the good times with a **1950's vibe, mini-golf and good food** at the snackbar. 9812 HONOR HIGHWAY, HONOR, 231-325-3413, CHERRYBOWLDRIVEIN.COM.

Train Depot

One of our favorite unsung hangouts. A sweet café (Station Espresso Bar). A décor shop (Urban Diversions). The light-filled EuroDog restaurant. Southwest corner of 8th and Woodmere Streets. Stop here before or after a hike on the Boardman Lake Trail.

52

53

Eat
Whitefish

This mellow-flavored, flaky fish
is the **menu icon of
the Great Lakes.**
There is no end to the delicious
ways Traverse City area restau-
rateurs prepare it. Discover your
favorite way at MyNorth.com.

GO TO FOOD AND WINE, DINING GUIDE.

Jet ski rental

Tool around **East Bay** on your own jet ski. **Thrill Rides** rents from a cabana on the beach in front of Sugar Beach Resort Hotel.

SEASONAL NUMBER 231-938-0100, TCBEACHES.COM.

54

55
ORYANA

Organic. Local foods. Gourmet. Hot topics nationwide, but they've been at the heart of Oryana food coop since 1973. We're especially fond of the café and the curry cashews. 10TH ST. & LAKE AVE., 231-947-0191, ORYANA.COOP.

Don't just look at the bay, float it, ride it, paddle it, in a kayak. Rent one at **Boardman Paddle & Pedal** (GARLAND ST., 231-944-1146, BOARDMANPADDLEANDPEDAL.COM) or **McLain Cycle** (2786 GARFIELD RD., 231-941-8855, MCLAINCYCLE.COM).

Kayak Rental

56

57

GRAND TRAVERSE
Lighthouse

Perched at the **tip of Leelanau Peninsula,** the Grand Traverse Lighthouse has shone for more than 150 years. **Climb the tower** (gorgeous!), check out the refurbished keeper's quarters. **Wander the beach.** NORTH OF NORTHPORT ON N. LIGHTHOUSE POINT RD., 231-386-7195, GRANDTRAVERSELIGHTHOUSE.COM.

Charter fishing
THE BAY

Hook into Grand Traverse Bay's **jumbo chinook, steelhead, coho, brown trout** and **lake trout** with the help of a wily charter fishing captain. Daydreamer Fishing Charters (231-218-5176) or Big Kahuna (231-946-7457).

58

Snorkeling
Class

A brief (but important) safety lesson and you are ready to **explore the underwater realm.** Class, equipment rental and sweet location tips at Scuba North (13380 S. WEST BAYSHORE DR., 231-947-2520, SCUBANORTH.COM).

59

60

METEOR SHOWER

When the Perseids meteor shower streaks our heavens the second week of August, find dark skies for **optimal viewing** on the beach at the tip of Old Mission Peninsula (M-37 NORTH TILL IT ENDS). Expect about **60 shooting stars per hour** at peak, generally August 12.

61

Rogers
OBSERVATORY

Saturn. The moon. Dark objects. Bright clusters. Friday and Saturday nights all year long, the Joseph H. Rogers Observatory invites the public to **scan the heavens** with a bonafide telescope. Take a looksee. 1753 BIRMLEY ROAD, NMC.EDU/ROGERSOBSERVATORY.

Fish Weir

When coho and chinook salmon swim up the Boardman River in the weeks around Labor Day, they funnel by the thousands into TC's fish weir, whereupon they are captured and trucked away (eventually becoming catfood). Strangely captivating to watch the **giant-fish traffic jam.** ON RIVERBANK, NORTHWEST OF FRONT ST. AND HALL ST.

62

Conservation preserves *galore*

Grand Traverse Regional Land Conservancy serves up about **20(!) publicly accessible nature preserves** within a half hour of Traverse City. Find one for your particular bliss (A lake? A stream? An island? A field? A forest?). 231-929-7911, GTRLC.ORG.

63

64

LAKE
DUBONNET

Reasons we love Lake Dubonnet. 1. Wild shoreline with few houses. 2. Fat bluegills, fighting smallmouth bass. 3. Close to TC. 4. Easy boat launch. Access about 3 miles north of Interlochen.

Kayak or hike
SKEGEMOG SWAMP

The **Skegemog Wildlife Area** spreads in a tangly, oozy, mysterious morass across 3,300 acres and along 7 miles of Lake Skegemog's eastern shore. **Get your dose of wild** on the marked trails or paddling the fringe in a shallow-bottomed boat. MAP AT GTRLC.ORG/PRESERVES/PRESERVEMAP.PHP.

65

66

Historic
WALKING TOUR

The **glamour and intrigue** of Traverse City's early lumber fortunes still reveal themselves in the proud and gracious **homes of 6th Street.** Pick up a tour map at the Grand Traverse Heritage Center. 322 6TH ST., 231-995-0313, GTHERITAGECENTER.ORG.

shop
FRONT STREET

Stroll and explore TC, one of the most vibrant small-town downtowns in America. Inventive boutiques, unexpected eateries, the ever-inspiring State Theatre and that gorgeous bay just a block away.

67

68

Experience a true heart-of-Traverse City moment. Head to Rounds Circle In and order up the **homemade** apple dumplings at this longtime (but newly nonsmoking) **locals' gathering spot.**

1033 E. EIGHTH ST., 231-941-4124.

Apple dumplings *at* Rounds diner

BLUE CHEESE
baguette

The Dalai Lama says the most important purpose of life is to seek happiness. Hence we suggest the blue cheese baguette at **Bay Bread Company.**

601 RANDOLPH ST., 231-922-8022.

69

70

Consider it a wine tour without the driving. Step into the **Cherry Stop,** right downtown, and sample among wines from several **local wineries.** 211 E. FRONT STREET, 231-929-3990, THECHERRYSTOP.COM.

local.
wine bar

71

Music
ON THE DECK

Essential components of summer: 1. Live music on a deck. 2. **Handcrafted brews.** 3. Friends gathered round. Get it at **North Peak Brewing Company** (and a tasty menu too). 400 W. FRONT ST., 231-941-7325. Music Tuesday through Saturday nights.

Traverse City
State Park

Since 1920, vacationers have **set up camp** at Traverse City State Park to soak up the sunny, sandy, watery goodness of Northern Michigan summer. **Fantastic beach** right there and just two miles to downtown TC's more urbane delights. $27 A NIGHT, 343 SITES, 231-922-5270.

Fairs, **Festivals** and Fun

73

Love a parade? Get starry-eyed at fireworks? Want to catch some live music? Get **the skinny on what's happening** in Traverse City at MYNORTH.COM, EVENTS.

74

The Michigan DNR website lists **57 inland lakes** in Grand Traverse County. Where does a fisherman begin? Well, anywhere, actually. But here are a few sure-bets: Arbutus Lake, Muncie Lake, Lake Dubonnet, and Long Lake. Cast into the shallows at dusk.

FISH
INLAND LAKES

Fish for carp

America is finally discovering what the rest of the world has long known: **carp are a crazy big fun fight** on the end of a fishing line. Cast the shallows of **Grand Traverse Bay** in June and July to feel the thrill.

75

76
casino

Get rich or have fun tryin'—the luxe **Turtle Creek Casino & Hotel** offers a big payoff even for nongamblers. **Watch the action** on the floor from the cocktail lounges above, hit the nightclub, **feast** in Bourbons 72 or **chill** on the patio by the rooftop garden. Gambler? You know what to do. 231-922-2WIN, TURTLECREEKCASINO.COM.

Aerie

Want an **elevated dining experience?** Ride the glass elevator to the 16th floor of the towering Grand Traverse Resort, where the **elegant but kid friendly** Aerie Restaurant & Lounge is ready to wow with an ever-changing seasonal menu, fine wines and a **panoramic view** of Grand Traverse Bay. Dinner nightly, plus Sunday brunch. 231-534-6800, GRANDTRAVERSERESORT.COM.

77

78

blossom days

Old Mission Peninsula's **cherry orchards** are **breathtaking at peak bloom time,** and so is the celebration they herald, Blossom Days—the annual May weekend when all of Old Mission's wineries uncork their newly released wines, open their barrels for tasting, offer winery tours and, since 1923, formally bless the blossoms. 231-223-4110, WINERIESOFOLDMISSION.COM.

79

The Village

Stroll the **gracious, historic grounds** of the 63-acre Village at Grand Traverse Commons, on the city's west side, then keep hiking into the **over 300 acres** of woodland trails that surround it. Head back to The Village and linger over a cup of organic, **fair trade coffee** at Higher Grounds Trading Company. 231-941-1900, THEVILLAGETC.COM

Boardman River
Nature Center

Bring the fam to **see, touch, smell and learn about Up North nature.** Inside the Boardman River Nature Center, you'll find an exhibit gallery, theater room, a craft area for kids, and countless fun and education programs, but the big highlight waits right outside the back door: a meandering, far-and-away-feeling **hike along the Boardman River.** NATUREISCALLING.ORG.

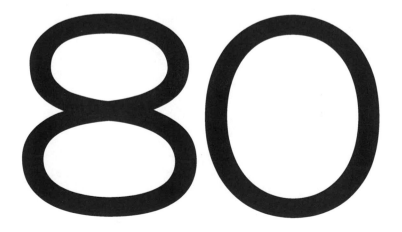

Parasail

Parasail above the **crystal clear waters** of East Grand Traverse Bay. You'll ease 400 or 800 feet in the air—your choice—with a partner or solo. **Big views, quiet blue sky** and an unforgettable summer memory in one. 231-929-PARA, TRAVERSEBAYPARASAIL.COM OR 231-929-3303, BREAKNWAVES.COM.

81

82

HOT AIR
Balloon

Catch sunrise or sunset from a hot air balloon. Grand Traverse Balloons will not only carry you to heaven in a hand basket (okay, balloon basket), they'll keep you aloft about an hour and break out some **bubbly to sip** while you watch the sun's show. 231-947-7433, GRANDTRAVERSEBALLOONS.

83

MERRY
Go Round

A parent's go-to **rainy day remedy:** take the tots for a whirl on the elaborately classic **carousel** that turns and tinkles vintage tunes inside the food court at the Grand Traverse Mall.

$1. 231-922-7722, GRANDTRAVERSEMALL.COM.

Top *of the park*

Toast the sunset from the **sweetest perch** in town: the **Beacon Lounge.** It sits on the top floor of the historic **Park Place Hotel,** overlooks Grand Traverse Bay and miles of downtown, and serves up **to-die-for martinis** and live entertainment Thursday, Friday and Saturday nights. 231-946-5000, PARK-PLACE-HOTEL.COM.

84

Antiquing

No dusty shelves or bric-a-brac here. The Traverse City area's dozen-plus antique shops and vintage stores are top-notch stops for the discriminating fan of the old fashioned. FIND HOURS AND ADDRESSES FOR EVERY ONE ON THE TRAIL: CLICK ON GRAND TRAVERSE COUNTY AT MI-ANTIQUES.COM.

85

86

POINT BETSIE LIGHTHOUSE

Locals say Point Betsie Lighthouse is the most photographed light on the Great Lakes. No doubt the light is **a photo-worthy stop,** and the beach is splendid, here at the southern end of the Manitou Passage. NORTH OF FRANKFORT ON M-22, 231-352-4915, POINTBETSIE.ORG.

OPEN SPACE

Go fly a kite, stick your nose in a novel, or people watch to your eyeball's content. No matter how you want to idle away a day, that **broad swath of verdant grass** between downtown and the West Bay beach—the aptly named Open Space—is the place to do it. CORNER OF UNION ST. AND GRANDVIEW PARKWAY.

87

88

Pyatt Lake
Nature Preserve

Former arm of East Grand Traverse Bay, now a uniquely Up North habitat—**wooded dune and swale**—Pyatt Lake Nature Preserve on Old Mission Peninsula is a **geological gem.** It's also one of the most peaceful places to sit by the water and watch the world *not* go by. MAP AND DIRECTIONS AT GTRLC.ORG.

AMERICAN SPOON FOODS

Butters! Jellies! Jams! Preserves! Before you pick from the plethora of jarred and bottled pleasures at Up North **food institution** American Spoon Foods, pick up a cracker and take a taste of whatever you fancy—free—at the Front Street shop's **extensive sample bar.** 231-935-4480, SPOON.COM.

89

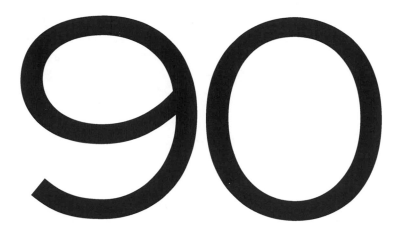

90

Dotting Long Lake's 4.5 square miles of surface water? **Small castaway-worthy islands:** South island is a natural preserve, Long, Picnic and Fox are designated parks, and all four are **open to the public.** Put in your boat at the Gilbert Park or Crescent Shore Road launches (both on the lake's west side).

LONG LAKE islands

SAND LAKES .
quiet area

More than **10 motor-free miles** of trails snake throughout this 3,000-acre preserve, meandering through hushed forests and around five oasislike lakes. **Camp anywhere here;** free camp cards are available at the Michigan Department of Natural Resource's Traverse City Field Office (970 EMERSON RD., 231-922-5280). Find Sand Lakes near Williamsburg, 3 miles south of M-72 on Broomhead Road.

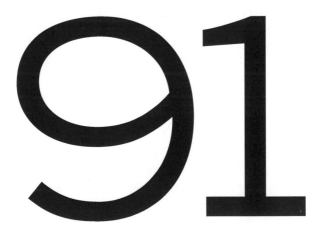

92

VASA trail

The namesake trail of Swedish King Gustav Vasa, the Vasa trail is **famous** for its national **cross-country and mountain bike races**, but locally, it's just plain loved for its **forest- and meadow-lined loops**—3K, 5K, 10K and 25K—the favorite stomping grounds for pleasure hikers, bikers, cross-country skiers and nature lovers. TRAVERSETRAILS.ORG.

Inland Seas **Schoolship**

Cruise Grand Traverse Bay and **learn something** along the way. The 77-foot tall-masted schooner invites aboard all kids, parents and learning buffs every summer for **brief sailing adventures** focused on hands-on science, maritime history, astronomy and the culture of the region. 231-271-3077, SCHOOLSHIP.ORG.

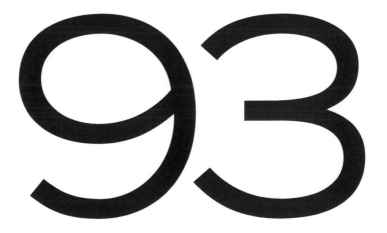

94

Smooch
THE MOOSE

TC's oldest continuously operated tavern, **Sleder's Family Tavern,** dates to 1882. Like its original bar—21 feet of solid mahogany—the historic eatery's **"good will is good business"** policy hasn't changed. Give a smooch to tavern mascot **Randolph the moose.** 231-947-9213, SLEDERS.COM.

RUN the Bayshore

This **annual Boston Marathon qualifier** race leads runners up and down Old Mission Peninsula's coastal orchard- and vineyard-framed roads—**a route so pretty** you could almost forget the pain in your aching legs. Almost. (Half marathon and 10K too). BAYSHOREMARATHON.COM.

95

96

Sushi
AT MEIJER

Used to be the Purple Cow was the must-stop spot while shopping at the Traverse City Meijer. These days, it's the sushi bar, where **uber-tasty** and tightly hand-rolled sushi is made fresh daily by a **bonafide sushi chef** and packaged to go. U.S. 31, SOUTH OF DOWNTOWN. 231-941-1543.

MUSIC HOUSE
Museum

The **early inventions** of musical master-minds await your eyes and ears at the **way-cooler-than-you'd-think** Music House Museum. **Take a tour** of the museum's rare antique musical instruments and machines—a giant Belgian dance organ, nickelodeons, music boxes, pipe organs among them—or pop in for a classic silent film backed by the Wurlitzer Theater Organ. 231-938-9300, MUSICHOUSE.ORG.

97

98

Laser Tag

Inside the 34,000 square foot entertainment mecca **Wilderness Crossing,** you'll find a two-story arena lit with black lights, clouded by haze, pumping with music and abuzz with kids and adults zapping each other in a **giggle- and shriek-fueled** game of laser tag. Up to 20 can play at a time. 231-943-9200, WILDERNESSCROSSING.COM.

TimberLanes

Throw some weight around—in the form of a 12-pound ball—at TimberLanes Bowling Center. **The fun doesn't stop after the frames:** for kids, this clean and well-lit spot sports a game room with six pool tables, pinball and a juke box, and for the big guys, a high-style billiards room. 231-947-2610, TIMBERLANESBOWLING.COM.

99

100

Reffitt
Nature Preserve

A **little known but easily accessed** nature preserve, the 83-acre George and Ada Reffitt Nature Preserve sits next to the TART trail, not far from the Traverse City State Park. To mosey its **1.7 mile loop trail and boardwalk,** mosey first to its trailhead immediately south of the railroad tracks on the east side of Three Mile Road near Parsons Road. GTRLC.ORG.

101

Old Town
Playhouse

Home of **Traverse City's community theater** world, the Old Town Playhouse has earned a place as a **much-loved** piece of the **TC arts vibe.** Catch a show. 148 E. 8TH STREET, 231-947-2210,

OLDTOWNPLAYHOUSE.COM